LEAVES ON THE TREE

All-Age Learning and Worship: Resources and Reflections

National Society/Church House Publishing
Church House, Great Smith Street, London SW1P 3NZ

ISBN 0 7151 4795 1

Published 1990 for the General Synod Board of Education jointly by the National Society and Church House Publishing.

Cover design by Bill Bruce

Printed in Great Britain by Martin's of Berwick.

Contents

Page

The Working Party

The members of the working party have wide and varied backgrounds of experience in working with all ages in different situations, both in this country and elsewhere. They are grateful for the help and advice given to them by colleagues working in youth and adult education, by parish priests, diocesan staffs and many members of congregations, of all ages.

Board of Education Working Party Members:

The Rev. Win Fish	Children's Adviser, diocese of Truro
Mrs Dorothy Jamal	Children's Officer, General Synod Board of Education (Chairman)
Sister Diane Lamb, CA	Children's Adviser, diocese of Lichfield
Miss Sharon Lovell	Children's Adviser, diocese of London
The Rev. Alison Lowe	Children's Adviser, diocese of Wakefield
The Rev. Peter Privett	Children's Adviser, diocese of Hereford

Consultative members:

Miss Ruth Ward	Youth Adviser, diocese of Southwark
The Rev. Anthony Sparham	Adult Link Director, diocese of Chester

Introduction

'All-age worship and learning? Toddler anarchy in the aisles,' 'disrupted discussions', 'noise and confusion', everything child-centred': these are some of the common fears, understood – but not held – by the writers of this book. We are hoping to provide some insights into what has become, within the Anglican Church and also in other denominations, an increasingly exciting and varied area, full of wonderful possibilities. It is an area in which many congregations are already finding rich new life. They are growing in faith and understanding; they are responding practically and imaginatively to the problems and possibilities that arise when all ages meet together for learning and worship.

The book is a direct response by the Board of Education to the many requests for help received from dioceses and parishes following the Report from the General Synod Board of Education *Children in the Way* (NS/CHP, £3.95), with its exploration and recommendation of a pilgrim model for Christian life and learning.

It was the letters, in fact, which gave us the inspiration for the format of this book. Why not – we thought – share the queries, the thoughts, the insights, in the hope that these letters, with accompanying comments and thoughts upon them, will inspire others to see how they can begin the sharing and learning together? So, in letters and answers, we are sharing our thinking and our work. Maybe you will find here the letter you would have written, or the one you did write. We hope that readers will find that the replies and comments speak to them and to their needs.

1

We have included many examples of activities and ideas sent by parishes throughout the country. As many people have asked for no public acknowledgement, we have not identified any of them by name. We do wish to express our deep gratitude to all the parishes and individuals who have contributed in this way. We also wish to thank all the Diocesan Advisers whose work in following up the Report has generated many splendid ideas, and has given a great number of people the opportunity to experience all-age learning and worship. Some of those ideas are to be found in these pages.

None of these suggestions are included in order that people should slavishly follow them. In worship and in learning, as in everything else, people are individuals. They have different needs and expectations; what 'works' in one place may not in another. But if this book is read, thought about and then used with imagination, with a willingness to try something that may be new and experimental, and with a knowledge of the local congregation, then we believe that readers will find their own ideas start to flow; a pattern of learning with all ages will begin to seem possible and desirable.

This is not a handbook for a 'one-off' event. Nor is it a definite collection of resources. It is, we hope, a book of *ideas* which will enable parishes to talk together, work together, worship together and plan their own programmes of on-going Christian education in which all-age learning together will take a vital and valued place.

The need for such Christian education and discussion has never been greater. The Decade of Evangelism with all its possibilities; the questions about Communion before Confirmation, which have yet to be resolved; both have profound implications for the pattern of parish learning and growth in faith. Our present-day concern for the environment and for creation in all its aspects is an all-age concern, needing to be translated into discussion, thought, prayer and action. Many other world and local issues are the obvious and proper concern of the Church.

We would add one plea. May we all realise that 'all-age learning' does *not* mean 'finding something that will keep the children occupied while the adults get on with the real business of learning or work'. May we consider the needs of *everyone*, and be open to the glorious possibilities of new discoveries and growth that are there for eighty-year-old faithful Mrs Jones, as they are for three-year-old Kylie Smith, when they meet with others as equals on the pilgrim path.

This is a book for those who believe that learning about faith, in

2

faith and with faith is a life-long process in which we are all children of God. It is a book by members of a group who have learned much together in writing it, and much more from the people of all ages with whom we are privileged to work.

Finally, the title of the book: *Leaves on the Tree*. This encapsulates all that we believe about the life and witness of all ages together on the Christian pilgrimage. It is a phrase from the hymn 'Immortal, invisible', and the relevant verse reads:

'To all life thou givest – to both great and small;
In all life thou livest, the true life of all;
We blossom and flourish as leaves on the tree,
And wither and perish – but nought changeth thee.'

Dorothy Jamal
Children's Officer,
General Synod Board of Education

3

1. What is 'All-Age Learning?'

'Dear Dorothy,
Why does the Church want adults and children to learn together when they are *not* expected to learn together in the secular world?'

It may be useful to define learning in order to put the 'all-age' aspect into context and to provide a framework to assist any evaluation after an event.

'Learning' is a process of many facets, all of which can be stimulated in many different ways.

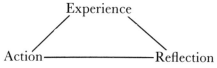

Three of the common denominators of the learning process are illustrated in the triangle above.

One part of the process is some kind of an *experience*, e.g. looking, listening, sharing or doing.

Reflection is another part of that process, during which one thinks about an experience and as a result may develop some new insight or understanding.

Action could be defined as 'what one does or doesn't do' as a result of the reflection and/or experience which has already taken place.

The fundamental principle is that *all* three aspects must have been present for learning to have taken place.

In the Church of England, and in other denominations over the past few years, this particular model of learning has become increasingly important when the need of all ages to learn together has been considered. Many Christians have come to believe that the value placed on each individual, regardless of age, must be reflected in the opportunities provided for them all to contribute and to share in each other's learning, each other's pilgrimage.

The words 'all age' will conjure up in every one of us a picture or idea of what we ourselves consider something 'all age' to be.

In this context we regard an all-age event or programme to be a process through which everybody in a congregation, whatever their age, can be engaged in a learning experience or an act of worship.

Any aspect of learning/worship usually involves some interaction and sharing with fellow learners/fellow worshippers, family, friends or colleagues.

Many adults involved in teaching will have recognised those moments of mutual interaction and will agree that, in the process of teaching youngsters, they have gained new insights themselves.

> '...My daughter's Sunday school party happened last year on Palm Sunday. As usual parents were also invited to take part.
>
> We divided into groups of mixed ages and my daughter decided to stay with me, to look at different events which occurred during that final week of our Lord's life and their implications today.
>
> Our group looked at Good Friday and as part of our thinking together my daughter and I rubbed a tile in the church which depicted the symbols of the crucifixion – the cross, the dice, the spear and the seamless robe.
>
> Normally I find it quite difficult to talk to my family about Christian things, but as we were rubbing the tile together my daughter began with the question "What were the dice for, mummy?" and we spoke together at great depth about Jesus and his love for us.
>
> How I wish the church would create more opportunities such as this where adults and children can learn alongside each other.'

(This letter can be found in full on p. 47)

In the gospel of Luke chapter 2, verse 47, we are told of the amazement with which the elders listened to the words of Jesus when he was twelve years old.

It is true that it is important for children to learn alongside other children, as indeed it is important for adults to be able to learn alongside other adults.

It is also true that children and adults need to be given opportunities to learn alongside each other, allowing interaction between the ages.

It is important that we *all*, as fellow Christians learning about our faith, are open to learn and share from and with each other.

As Nigel Forde puts it in his script for the video *Children in the Way* (National Society):

> 'They may not have the knowledge we possess
> So the Holy Spirit has to shift much less
> In terms of intellectual debris
> Than perhaps he might with you. Or you. Or me.'

and:

> 'Life is a journey. "Gosh!" you say, "that's new!"
> Well – sorry if it's trite, but it *is* true.
> You can stride out smug, confident, alone,
> And let your children find the long way home,
> Or you can stay and help them stay on course
> With that fragment of map that's only yours;
> While they have sections that you've never seen,
> Which might help you across the odd ravine.'

There are already examples in our churches of all ages being involved in an activity together: for instance, the choir. This could be developed into an *all-age learning experience* by allowing time during choir practice for all the members to think and talk about the meaning of the words they are singing. This could then be developed, occasionally, in the *Sunday* worship by one or two of the choir sharing their insights when the hymn is announced, and by giving time for any of the congregation to contribute theirs. This model of working could be used in other areas of church life.

When we use any phrase which contains the words 'all age', it is easy to think of all the untried and untested ideas of merging everybody into an activity. It may be hard to believe it is possible to cater for everybody all the time.

'Dear Dorothy,

I am extremely keen to have an all-age event held in my parish, BUT I visited a neighbouring church to see how they did it and the result was total chaos.

Please could you tell me how to plan such an event and let me have any guidelines?'

When planning an all-age event it is vital that you ask yourself very carefully indeed:

WHY are you planning this event?
HOW are you going to plan it?
WHO is involved in the planning and the event itself?
WHAT will be the results in terms of an on-going programme of learning?

When planning an event also you need to be clear about:

WHAT are you aiming to achieve?
WHAT are your objectives?
HOW will you best achieve them?

Being quite clear about these three aspects of the event will help you to decide on its content and format.

It is also vital to build into the day time when those taking part can *evaluate* what has been happening. This, ideally, means giving them time to reflect on what they have learned and to share with each other. The feedback needs to be discussed by those who *were* involved in the planning and by those who *will* be involved in planning *future* events. From such evaluations it could be possible to prepare an all-age programme/policy/strategy for the parish.

Some questions to ask when planning an all-age event:

Who will decide on the theme?
How to introduce the theme?
How can people easily introduce themselves to each other?
Is worship to be included?
Who will lead the worship?
How will it fit in?
What time of the year is it?
Publicity?
Food?
Transport?
Venue?

Toilets?

Budget?

Financial implications?

Remember that the timing and the appropriateness of the event, being all-age, is as crucial as the design and content itself.

It is the process and content of learning and worship which makes it a positive or negative experience and a workable or non-workable one.

All-age learning does not mean children's events, nor activities that adults are encouraged to join in, but a selection of activities suitable and appropriate for *everybody* in accordance with the aims and objectives of the event. We constantly need to ask what we are aiming for and what is the best way of achieving this. This means that those who are taking part will have to be considered as individual people with different needs.

Many people see all-age activities as all ages meeting together every week to do the same thing. BUT there are other possibilities.

For instance:

(a)   People grouped according to ages: adults in one group, teenagers in another, children in another.

Each group to engage in a task.

All groups come together to share and participate in each others' activities.

(b)   All ages grouped together in separate groups: (say) five groups comprising a mixture of ages.

Each group to engage in an activity or task.

All groups then come together to share and participate in each others' activities.

(c)   All ages come together as one body.

Large group engages in the same activity/task.

Ideally we can work towards an all-age event which is also *planned* by all ages.

Whoever does plan and design the all-age activity needs to take special care in matching individuals to groups and tasks. For instance, it would not be wise to put an adult, teenager or child into a group which requires reading or writing if that person is known to have difficulty with these skills. It is therefore always good to provide an element of *choice* wherever possible in order that people will feel comfortable with the task.

So often great assumptions are made about what adults should know or do know – as indeed great assumptions are also made about how little children know and how little they have experienced. It is possible that a ten-year-old child who has attended church since birth has, in fact, a wider experience and knowledge of the Christian faith than a 35-year-old adult who has attended church for one year. Neither can be said to have a greater, better or deeper faith than the other. They are merely 'different'.

Results can sometimes be achieved through an all-age learning experience which are totally unpredictable, unexpected and unplanned – and which could have been achieved in no other way. Why is this so?

Conversations, sharing of ideas, thoughts and feelings all happen naturally in people's own time, at their own pace and, most important of all, in their own way.

Because all-age learning structures tend to be flexible, everybody has more opportunities to relate and interact at his or her own level of understanding and development.

As all ages are engaged in a task together, the barriers, assumptions and stereotypes which go with being adult, teenage or a child become less apparent and gradually break down.

Eventually people are able to lose their presuppositions about the various age groups, their abilities and experiences.

As all these assumptions, stereotypes and barriers are broken down, so each one of us acquires the opportunity to discover, explore and acknowledge our own gifts and the gifts of others. All ages have the opportunity, perhaps for the first time, to be in fellowship with each other, as opposed to being in a fellowship restricted by boundaries of age.

Through this process, individuals learn not only to recognise gifts in others, but to value others as they are, not for what they know or because they fit into a particular category.

An all-age experience, therefore, will take place if

(a) All those engaging in the activity are seen as of equal value in the eyes of one another;

(b) all are seen as having a contribution to make;

(c) within the group each individual finds mutual affirmation, respect, appreciation and friendship.

If all-age learning is to take place, however, we must be prepared to let our expectations be broad and to be ready for the unpredictable.

9

When participating in an all-age activity it is essential that we have an open mind. We must have the willingness to be open to others: their thoughts, feelings and experiences.

Only by being 'open' in this way are we able to benefit from the 'fusion' process whereby the thoughts and words of others spark off an idea, thought or concept in us. It may be a totally new idea, or a slight modification of an old one. It may even be a reminder of an insight we had forgotten. If we think, 'Oh, she's only a child, what does she know?' our minds are still closed. If our minds are open, we may hear something that could change our attitude to life.

A thought to ponder:

> 'I thought about the great desire among friends and colleagues and travellers who meet on the road to share what they know, what they have seen and imagined.
>
> Not to have a shared understanding but to share what one has come to understand. In such an atmosphere of mutual regard, in which each can roll out his/her maps with no fear of contradiction or suspicion of theft, it is possible to imagine the long graceful strides of human history.'

(from *Arctic Dreams* by Barry Lopez)

SUMMARY OF IDEAS FOR LEARNING TOGETHER

This chapter looks at what all-age learning is and what it can do for people. It includes thoughts about aims and objectives, and reflections and general thinking to do *before* planning, while planning and afterwards.

Page 5: A mother's account of learning with her daughter

Things to do Have an all-age activity day, for instance Mothering Sunday, Palm Sunday. Let mixed ages, in groups, explore together the symbols we have that show love for each other in a family: a look, a hug, giving birthday cards, keeping photographs, etc. Discuss ways in which we use symbols to express how we feel about God's love, and explore the church for symbols – candles, cross, symbols of the Passion, etc. Work in art, collage, models, poetry, banners can follow and be exhibited by the leader or presented in worship.

Page 6: The choir as an example of all ages involved together
Things to do It may not be easy, but the choir can be a way in to involve everyone in thinking about music and its place in worship. Words of hymns, the need for practice, how music affects us, choice of hymns for baptisms, weddings, funerals, stories of some of the hymns: all are 'starter' ideas. Plan an evening or an afternoon with the choir and organist/choir leader to involve everyone in this thinking and to learn and enjoy a range of music together.

Page 7: Planning an event
The Midland Diocesan Advisers have produced an excellent booklet called *Signposts on the Way*, giving detailed ideas for all-age events – see Resources list on page 64, and note page 45 for details of further information about parachute games. It also gives details of activities for a day event and useful planning ideas.

2. Implications for Worship

'Dear Dorothy,

I was recently able to be involved in a diocesan event in which all ages took part in various workshops and activities. I took part in conversation and work with children and adults, and saw how valuable the day was for us all. However, my own parish is a small rural one – no one came with me to the event. The only thing they come to is our Sunday Eucharist. Can you tell me how I can involve all ages in *that* and introduce into it opportunities for learning?'

Diocesan events often lead people to look again at their parish situation, sometimes in despair, sometimes with real hope of change and growth. One way to do this might be to encourage the congregation, or a smaller group – the PCC or worship group, for example – to consider the following points:

1. In what ways can we work so that there will be a deeper understanding by all ages of the overall pattern and constituent parts of the Eucharist?

2. What skills in prayer, use of silence, use of our building, music, symbols, etc. do we need to develop?

3. How can we help each individual, whatever that person's age, to be absorbed in, feel part of, be caught up in the action that belongs to the whole community?

To start where people are is often the wisest thing to do – often it is the only way to start any parish education with a regular pattern. The rubrics for the ASB, for example, allow considerable latitude in the format of the liturgy, and advantage is not always taken of this. For example, note 20 on page 115 of the ASB allows the Peace and Offertory to take place at other points than those indicated in the rubrics.

In addition it is possible to use many points of the service as learning opportunities. Chapter 1 of this book suggests a way to introduce some thinking about the hymns being sung. Occasionally it could be helpful for people to have some information about the writer of a particular hymn, or the story behind the hymn (some hymns, such as 'Rock of Ages' or the modern hymns of Brian Wren, were written after or during particular events in life). The same is true of many hymn tunes, and the sharing of such knowledge can enrich, enliven and deepen the meaning of a hymn. In some parishes once a month, or on certain Sundays in the year, people are encouraged to choose a hymn and to say something about their choice. This can help the congregation to realise the relevance of the theme, the significance of the readings for that week, and how the hymns fit in – or don't! It also enables people to share a little of their own story (see the discussion on story in Chapter 3).

There are various points in the Eucharist where silence is indicated as a possible response. It is a pity that more congregations of all ages are not enabled and encouraged and taught to discover how silence may be used. For many people it is an uncomfortable time; they become guilty about wandering thoughts, or anxious that their child shall not make a noise. Others, trying to use the silence to pray, find it unsatisfactorily short, or feel a lack of any clear idea how to respond.

Silence is something that all ages can share, and helping people to focus on a symbol, a window, a part of the building can help. Introducing silence with a sentence, a question, a text, a thought, or leading into it with music, can help people to use it more meaningfully. Sometimes people even wonder if it is right to move, whether they must kneel, or sit, or what during a silence – so some help with feeling comfortable and knowing what to expect from your body, your mind and spirit is important. It is also necessary to help people to understand the concept of listening in the silence. For many, that has to be first of all becoming used to hearing the sounds of the building, their neighbours' movements, the sounds from the outside, before they become aware that they can listen to God speaking.

The Ministry of the Word offers many possibilities for the way in which the readings are presented and the sermon space is used. Later in this chapter we give ideas for the use of the building at this point of the service, but one of the most important and fundamental things, however you may plan to present the reading, is to ensure that all who read – whatever their age – are well-trained. They must be able to give of their best, with confidence about difficult words, peculiar names and so forth, and they must be able to be clearly heard. Some parishes ask all who are to read during the next month to meet after a service or at some other time, to practise together, to realise the importance of what they are doing, to look at the readings, ask questions, and to enter into the drama and delight of presenting the biblical material to others. This in itself can be an all-age learning experience. *The Dramatised Bible* (Marshall Pickering), which arranges the actual text for various voices, could be a great help to parishes trying to present readings in different ways.

There are parishes that regularly involve families at the time of the intercessions so that the adults, young people and children (and often grandparents, or aunt, uncle, parent and child) plan this together. In some churches an organisation such as the Mothers' Union takes a turn and involves some of their families – in other churches members of the choir do this. As with the readings, practical help with voice production and speed of delivery is essential. It is also possible to help people to vary the ways in which the intercessions are presented; for help with this, see Chapter 7, on Resources.

The exchanging of the Peace is for some congregations a time of great joy and symbolism. For others it is a time of acute embarrassment and often painful anticipation that can detract from all that happens before the Peace is offered. Some congregations and ministers have treated this with sensitivity. The significance is regularly taught, and people are reminded that a smile, with no physical contact, can for many be a 'sign of peace' and will be accepted by others as such. This is a time in some churches where, if the children have gone out for particular learning together, they return and initiate with the minister the passing of the Peace. It is a time when it is possible for all ages to be helped to be aware not only of all the symbolism and history and meaning of the words and actions, but also helped to be understanding and aware of the needs and responses of others.

14

The Offertory procession could be a time of great visual significance and teaching. All too often in some churches it is a self-conscious shamble up the aisle to present the gifts of bread, wine, money and ourselves in an action scarcely seen or recognised by many of the people present. The words of thanks and praise are often said hastily and all the possibilities for a great acclamation, for symbol and wonder, are lost. Here at the centre of the Eucharist we are giving to God all that he has given to us, offering all that we are that we might become all that he would make us – this is a moment week by week when we can help people to grasp something of the mystery and joy, the love and thanksgiving.

The practice in many churches of asking people as they arrive, or after they are seated, 'Would you like to take up the bread and wine?' does not seem the best way to achieve this. As with all parts of worship, the taking-up of the gifts needs a time of thought for those involved, and some understanding of what they are doing on behalf of everyone. It is a place for all-age learning, both before in the planning and at the time of the Offertory – not perhaps every week, but at regular intervals throughout the year. The way the gifts are presented needs to be discussed. Churches whose monetary offerings are collected in a bowl at the back of the church, or mainly through covenants, may need to think how to make this a visible part of the total offering of *all* the people week by week, in which all ages can share.

For some adults and for many children the Eucharistic prayer loses a great deal of its story, its significance and its symbolism because there is little opportunity for the congregation to be involved in it. *Patterns for Worship*, the 1989 Report by the Liturgical Commission (CHP), gives various examples of the prayer with a variety of responses and acclamations for the people. Some churches have tried modelling this part of the Eucharist on the Jewish Passover meal with its 'telling of the story'. It could be possible to have a child or adult asking, as the declaration is made: 'It is right to give thanks and praise', 'Why is it right to give thanks and praise?' – and then have the response from the priest, 'It is indeed right...' and the people responding with the next 'reason' – 'For He is your living word... formed us in your own image'. On some occasions the next section also could be treated similarly – 'Through him you have freed us from the slavery of sin...a people for your own possession'.

There are many other ways which will become apparent to people once the opportunity is given to think about what is happening week by week. Ideas from all ages will enable congregations to vary, deepen and enrich their worship, within the context of the Eucharist or whatever is the pattern of their normal Sunday worship.

Much of the worship in this country takes place in buildings about which many of the worshippers, of all ages, know very little. It is possible to use the buildings in the context of worship for learning. They are usually our greatest resource for all-age learning activities. Within a normal Sunday service, Eucharist or other, it is possible to use the building in imaginative and helpful ways.

As acknowledged in *Patterns for Worship*, 'the church family at worship should acknowledge the presence and gifts of children and be open to inter-generational learning and experience of worship'. One way of doing this is to make a more imaginative use of the building in which a congregation worships.

Patterns for Worship emphasises the poor way in which the Bible is often read in churches; using the building could mean having different readings of the Bible with several voices from different parts of the church. We could abandon the use of the lectern and place a reader in the pulpit, among the congregation, in the choir, a gallery, or at some other point that links with the reading – such as by the altar, the font, a window.

Prayer and intercessions can involve use of various parts of the building. For instance, a war memorial or memorial plaque, or window, could be a focal point to lead into silent prayer and meditation on All Souls', All Saints', or Remembrance Day. Prayers could be led from the font or the door when praying for the newly baptised, those about to be confirmed, or the Church worldwide.

Pillars are a marvellous visual symbol of strength and support and can be used as such for meditation. Windows speak of light, colour, people, of looking outwards and inwards. Church flowers often have symbolic meaning, or a significance in their colour and shapes. A congregation can be asked sometimes to look down, or look up to the roof, to look around the building for 10-15 minutes using 'guide' cards (see the Resources in Chapter 7), and explore the building instead of a sermon, or to come back and discuss their findings with a neighbour. A focus on the building, in words or silence, could conclude the time thus spent.

A parish day could be organised, based on the church, and a variety of activities offered within its walls. Such a day could be structured with the help of various cards and books available (see Resources list) and different media used to explore the church. A similar day might involve setting up groups to work within the church on themes such as flower arranging, music, drama, art, the spoken word, a study of stained glass, brasses, light, symbols. Such days would involve sharing lunch together, a time for discussion, and sharing of ideas, possibly within the context of worship, which might be in the context of a Eucharist, or could be worship at the end of the day which draws together some of the various activities and thinking of the group.

> 'I'd love to be able to say I welcome children in our church each week, but I really cannot tolerate the way that small children are allowed to crawl all over the place and often scream and shout. I like some quiet in worship and I can't understand why parents don't realise that church isn't the place for this kind of behaviour. Surely it should be possible for children to be kept quiet in the service?'

For some churches the difficult thing is to get any children into the church at all! For others the problem is knowing what to do when they've got them there. The answer to the question, 'How do we expect children to behave in church?' usually depends on our answer to the question 'Why do we want children in church?' If we want them there because we believe they have as much right as we have to be there, equal members in their own right, then we shall want them to share our activities there as fully as possible. The main activity will be worship, so surely we shall want them to learn, week by week, the pattern of worship, to become familiar with the movements, the actions, the words.

Of course, there will be times when the youngest children want to express their feelings by loud comment or by crying. It is important to make it easy for parents to take them out without embarrassment. One way might be to have members of the congregation as 'aunt' or 'uncle', to sit near or with them, to help at such 'crises' and share responsibility for worship with the family. To have children in church and encourage them to regard it merely as a play space is not necessarily the most helpful attitude for the parents, the children or the rest of the congregation. Those people who find it difficult to accept the presence of children in worship are more likely to see the value and the rightness of their presence if they can also discern an attempt being made to help the children to be part of what is happening and to learn week by week. In the words of John Westerhoff:

> 'If we really love our children, if we really want them to grow in Christian faith, we need to spend more time looking at our own growth in faith.'

It is when children become 'our children' to a congregation that such growth can really begin for everyone.

Some parishes have experimented with a mid-week service in the early evening and have brought all ages together in a 'family service' type of service. The possibilities, practicalities, problems and pitfalls of 'family services' are dealt with fairly extensively in *Patterns for Worship*. For some parishes they have proved to be the way to enable children and adults to come together and share fully in worship, when this has not been possible in the Eucharist. For other parishes the 'family service' means a Communion service in which all are given some opportunities to share in readings, taking up the Offertory and so on.

Whatever is being tried, it seems vital to keep in mind the needs of an all-age congregation. Having children present does not mean watering everything down, nor does it give a licence for toddler anarchy in and out of the pews. If we really want our children, young people and adults to share worship, then we must help the youngest and the oldest to experience all the rich variety of worship that is possible. If worship is to be something worthy, something that will enable people of all ages to grow in faith and understanding, it must enable them to enter into awe and wonder, delight and discovery! It must have at its heart the mystery of love. It must help even the youngest present to know an atmosphere of peace and expectancy, of times of silence and times of joyous acclamation. All the richness of our church buildings with their symbols, colour, their 'loneliness', their austerity, their flowers and light, their history, their contemporary style, their architecture and art, their beauty and sometimes their sad neglect must be used if our worship is to be the worship of all ages and of all the ages.

Worship should be a time, as a parishioner in a Yorkshire church said, when 'we are given permission to be ourselves, together'. We should expect from the youngest of us present a gradual recognition of all this; we should expect from the oldest of us present a gradual recognition that this may only be fully experienced when all ages worship together.

Worship needs to give opportunities for all present to be able to enter in fully at some point. These will not be the same points for everyone and no-one should be made to feel guilty because they do not feel able to participate fully *all* the time. At a lecture given at the European Conference on Christian Education in Stirling (1989), John Westerhoff said:

> 'Each week, the baptised share a need to go on a journey. Black and white, women and men, old and young, poor and rich, they leave their homes and labours as persons who are aware that they have denied and distorted their baptismal covenant and thereby have experienced brokenness and incompleteness. Bringing their lives and "world" with them, they come to hear and respond to God's healing Word, to offer their broken and incomplete lives as a sacrifice holy and acceptable to God, to make Eucharist for God's reconciling love, to be reconstituted as Christ's body and to be taken up into the reign of God so that they might return to the world bringing God's reign with them and being Christ's healing, reconciling presence wherever they live and work.

> 'While this image of the Christian's weekly journey surely makes theological and liturgical sense, it may not correspond with our experience. We all know those who regularly attend the Sunday liturgy of the Church, but rarely experience transformation in their perceptions, convictions and commitments, who rarely receive the gifts of healing and wholeness, who rarely are enabled and empowered to be more faithful in daily life and work.'

SUMMARY OF IDEAS FOR LEARNING TOGETHER

This chapter looks at the implications of all-age learning for worship. One letter sets a scene common in many parishes: worship *is* the only time when it seems possible to get all ages together. The chapter gives *explicit* suggestions for all parts of the Eucharist. These ideas, linked with suggested resources, should enable leaders of worship to think how they can work with the building, the liturgy, the worshippers in more imaginative and helpful ways.

3. Glimpses of the Divine

'Dear Dorothy,
I was in the garden the other evening enjoying some peace and quiet. Our neighbour came out of her kitchen door, took one look at the magnificent evening sky and gave a great shriek of delight. This was followed by a series of cartwheels around the garden, finishing with her lying back in an exhausted heap on the lawn. I came out of hiding, applauding and shouting "Bravo!" There was a brief shock of embarrassment which was dissolved by a smile, followed by giggles and laughter from both of us.

I thought afterwards, that here was a glimpse of the nature of the divine.

At the heart of the universe is a delight in the wonder and beauty of created things.

At the heart of the universe is one who dances for joy.

At the heart of the universe is a silence, a giggle and laughter...'

The purpose of spirituality is to enable us to catch a glimpse of the divine, to raise up our humanity so that it becomes divine and to catch that which is divine and make it human.

During the Eucharist we use the words:
'All things come from you and of your own do we give you'
and
'...it is our duty and our joy, at all times and in all places, to give you thanks and praise.'

All times, all places, all things, the whole of the created order: these are the vehicles and means of knowing and seeing God.

The inclusion of the all-age element in learning and worship reinforces this truth. It clearly proclaims that the whole range of human experience is available to us so that we can explore together and rejoice in the manifold ways in which God reveals truth. One way in which we grow spiritually is to realise the value of 'interdependence'. When times, people and places connect for us, then spiritual sparks begin to fly.

These are the moments of vision, of perception, of revelation...

These are the moments of profound silence and joy...

These are the moments of 'Oh, yes, I see...'

These are glimpses of heaven and signs of the kingdom...

These are moments that are often fragmentary and fragile...

These are gifts, and we have them by the grace of God.

Glimpses of the divine are deeply precious and personal and we often want to keep them so, but set alongside this is often a great desire to share the treasure with others.

> 'Dear Dorothy,
> My wife's grandmother died some time ago. Both our children attended the funeral and the youngest, who was six, became extremely angry when the undertaker tried to persuade him not to enter the crematorium after the church service. "She's MY great-grandma..." he shouted defiantly. He also insisted that he be included in the scattering of the ashes a few days later.
>
> There were times when we wondered about the wisdom of including him so fully. Outwardly he resembled a crushed leaf but we realised that he was entitled to grieve like the rest of us and to exclude him would have been inhuman. During that time we laughed and cried as we remembered the life of Grandma and all that she meant to us...It was a most religious time.'

Our life experience is of fundamental importance in our spiritual journey. The times of transition, of birth, of growth, of falling in love and of death are occasions when many people make connections with the divine. There need to be safe places where people of all ages can tell their story of these times and, in so doing, begin to order and make sense of the events. Large formal church services are probably not the appropriate setting for this. For some it will be done within the family; for others the stories of such times will be explored with friends. Church house-groups have an enormous potential as the place where stories of all ages can be heard, explored and celebrated.

The *Children in the Way* Report gave us the image of the Pilgrimage: people of different ages travelling the road together. If we are committed to travelling together, then I need to hear your story and you need to hear mine. As we listen to each other, your story may impinge on mine. Perhaps it will alter it and enlarge it. It may mean that I have to rethink and release some parts of my story that I once held dear. Of course, the same may happen to you; it's all part of the pilgrimage.

One of the stages in our Christian spiritual journey is the ability to test our experience, not only against one another but also against that of our ancestors in the faith.

All through the Bible runs a pattern of pilgrimage and movement. God seems to be constantly moving people on and enlarging the boundaries.

The Old Testament begins with a revelation to a small tribe of Middle Eastern nomads; it ends with a picture of all the nations being called to Mount Zion. The New Testament continues the theme; all the created order is reconciled in Christ and men, women and children are called to co-operate and proclaim this great truth.

> 'The biblical story is a symbolic narrative...that is why it enlightens us about ourselves and fosters our growth...It offers meanings on various levels and enriches our lives in countless ways...'
> (*Bringing Up Children in the Christian Faith*, John Westerhoff)

Westerhoff goes on to warn against the dangers of using the biblical story to moralise or indoctrinate, as this does a great injustice to the material. What we need to do is simply tell the story so that we can make our own connections. We need to tell the biblical stories again, imaginatively and with life, so that we see the prototypes and patterns by which we can identify our own experiences.

The nature of the biblical story depends upon action and response.

22

Much of the material was originally passed on by word of mouth. People told each other stories. We need to recover these elements. In so doing we enrich our spirituality.

Our western society seems to have lost the art of live storytelling. Many dramas are presented to us on TV, in the cinema and the theatre, but all too often these are passive activities. We sit and watch without taking part. The use of community theatre and community arts projects, however, are slowly giving people back skills so that they can present their own story and experience.

Poetry, dance, craft, drama, mime, art and music should belong to everyone. These are the raw materials with which stories are told...and these are the raw materials of worship. They are the raw materials in which we express our spirituality. We need to re-skill ourselves and really believe that we can sing, move, dance and create...

All-age learning and worship work provides excellent opportunities to use all the creative arts to experience the truths of the biblical story and to set alongside these experiences and stories of ourselves, whatever our age. (Look, for instance, at the description of icon-making in Chapter 6, and at the resources highlighted from this present chapter in the summary on page 27.)

Alongside this is the great spiritual need to educate and develop the imagination. In a world with a growing emphasis on consumerism, task-oriented work, and the achievement of objectives, there is a real danger that the cost will be fewer dreamers and visionaries. Our spirituality is dependent upon our having space to dream dreams, to proclaim messages and to see visions.

> 'I will pour out my spirit on everyone...your sons and daughters will proclaim my message, your old men will have dreams and your young men will see visions...'
>
> (Joel 2.28)

Ritual and symbolic actions are of prime importance in our spiritual journey.

> 'Ritual emerges from and brings into being the symbols by which life is made meaningful. The language of faith which conveys our perceptions is the language of symbolic actions. We kiss our children not only because we love them but so that we can love them...we make believe so that we may believe...'
>
> (*Bringing up Children in the Christian Faith*)

23

'Dear Dorothy,

We knew another Dorothy who, in her mid-fifties, died of cancer. Her husband buried her ashes in the Pyrenees because she had many associations with that area. We decided to visit the place and our two children, aged 5 and 7, thought the idea of a camping holiday was great.

On our way we stopped off at Chartres and visited the cathedral.

Inside, our five-year-old son's attention was taken by a statue of Mary surrounded by hundreds of lit candles.

"What's that?" he enquired.

"People come here to say prayers," I replied, "and then they light a candle to remind them of their prayer."

We moved on and after a while I realised that my son wasn't with us. I looked back to see him still with the statue. He went to the pile of unlit candles, took one, lit it and placed it with the others. Then he stood perfectly still and gazed at the Madonna.

"What are you doing?" I whispered.

"Ssh!" he said, "I'm lighting a candle for Dorothy."

As I write the same rush to breathe creases me and tears well into my eyes. I remember putting my hand into his and standing with him in silence.'

All-age work should provide many opportunities for adults to share with children the rich spiritual inheritance of the ages. When these traditions are shared with sincerity and meaning, children are only too willing to take them and make them their own. They often give them back to the adults with new understanding that enriches and enlarges the original intention.

Children and adults need to have opportunities to experience a richness and variety of traditions, in order to build up for themselves a treasury of spiritual resources. The aim is not to manipulate or dominate. The resources are not ends in themselves; they are but recipes and ingredients to enable prayer. They are there to help us to open a window towards God.

Today we are increasingly aware of expectations, pressure, business. Many adults and young people seem to have few opportunities for stillness, quietness and silence.

24

Time given to silence and reflection has been found to benefit greatly both adults and children. At a recent all-age day on the theme of recreation, both adults and children spent time doing simple breathing exercises, reflecting on the breath of God coming in and going out of them. Questions such as 'What have we learned today?' 'What has been important for you today?' can provide opportunities for reflection and contemplation.

Our spiritual growth is not only about our glimpses into heaven and the ability to share the stories of those glimpses. It must also deal with the ways that those glimpses impinge upon our actions.

A vital part of the reflecting experience must include ideas for action, changes of behaviour, both now and in the future.

A parish recently spent a weekend together exploring the doctrine of creation and green issues: 'God's world, Our world'. The worship which included all ages was profound, the implications for future behaviour equally so. Ideas for action and for changes in behaviour came from adults and children alike.

At a recent family service the preacher was describing the situation in the New Testament Corinthian church, dwelling on the arguments and divisions in its congregation. He threw in a rhetorical question (a dangerous thing to do in a family service): 'Well, what can you do when people are like that?'

A six-year-old sitting near the front at once thrust his hand up and said simply and directly, 'People need to sit down and talk it over and try to be friends again.' His comment stopped the sermon and the whole congregation present saw the point of this for their own behaviour. All-age work commits us to find ways where all ages can be part of the decision-making process, finding ways to change and act together.

The image of a journey is often used to describe spiritual growth. It ends, as it begins, with the goodness of God – with the richness and variety of creation and with the richness and variety of human relationships.

Through this richness and diversity we journey towards wholeness, the integration of body, mind and spirit, not only for ourselves but for others. The aim of our journey is to develop a community, a belonging, a sense of unity. Our journey is towards God.

'Dear Dorothy,
I was in a group of people the other day and the discussion got around to the doctrine of the Trinity. I'm not quite sure why, but it did. There was some talk about community and the word interdependence was mentioned several times.

I then found myself saying...

"It all has to do with the Trinity. God cannot be God without the relationships within. The Father cannot be Father without the Son and the Spirit. The Son cannot be the Son without the Father and the Spirit. The Spirit cannot be the Spirit without the Father and the Son. They all need each other to be God, they have to be interdependent."

I then realised that this was the thinking behind all-age learning and worship. The child, the teenager, the adult, all need to relate to each other in order to be themselves. For them to be themselves they must be interdependent.

In fact all-age learning and worship is a reflection of the Trinity and the Trinity is a reflection of all-age learning and worship.'

SUMMARY OF IDEAS FOR LEARNING TOGETHER

This chapter encourages us to think about spirituality through the whole of our life, to encourage people of all ages and stages to be aware of each other's stories and their importance.

Page 22: House groups

People of all ages could be encouraged to meet not just for a period of study or prayer, but to share their spiritual journey, their stories. This can be done by helping each person to draw a life chart, showing significant points, and to talk about it to another or others. If this were done on a parish day, and people encouraged to talk about where they see themselves now and their particular needs in their Christian life, they could then go into arranged groups for Bible work, painting icons, prayer or meditation, singing and so on, or else continue talking with another or others.

Page 23:   Storytelling and use of creative arts
There are many suggestions in Chapter 6 of ways in which these can happen. There needs to be regular opportunity for people to express in different media their feelings and thoughts, faith and understanding. Sometimes a day or weekend away in a conference centre, religious house, in another parish can be the start of shared expertise and enlarged vision.

Page 25:   Silence
Children enjoy 'creative silence' and love to share it with adults. The use of a candle, a piece of pottery, driftwood, flowers, a picture, a banner or a window in the church can provide a valuable focus.

Page 25:   The six-year-old's comment reminds us that the presence of children leads to opportunities for deep and shared learning and action.

4. Implications for Life and Living

'Dear Dorothy,
My parish church and the local Methodist chapel organised what we called a "Chapel-Church Fun Day". Our
intent was a rather vague hope that the two Christian
congregations would get to know and trust one another
more with a view to growing closer together in life and
worship. But could this be a beginning to looking at what
we do from an "all-age learning" perspective? Certainly
young Phillip taught some of us older fogies how to have
fun with frisbies without too much strain on the arthritis!'

Such things can indeed be a good beginning. Just playing, talking and
responding together in an informal atmosphere can help us to see one
another more perceptively and with a deepened appreciation. A few
moments of talk at the end of the day around a camp-fire or with a
warm drink as the participants tell one another their stories of the day
is a useful and happy exercise. Certainly, as happened in one
community, a little 'next time' group could be formed from those of
different ages involved in the day, to plan further events: an All-Age
Ideas Group in which different perceptions and needs could be heard
and employed. For example, from such a context of fellowship and
reflection could arise an All-Age Activity Day when all ages share
their talents and perceptions, their enthusiasms and questions as they
learn and experience together within a community of faith. Such a
Day, sensitively planned, could also draw upon the talents and

experience of the wider community. It could be a gentle means of witness as well, by being open to youngsters and adults in the wider neighbourhood. Nothing but benefit can come to a church which is open not only to welcoming the neighbourhood without strings attached, but also to enlisting the help and wisdom of people other than its own immediate membership.

An activity day or event might take as its theme a contemporary concern such as family life, health or life expectations: it could explore, against the background of the Gospel and the experience of the Church, such problems as loneliness, unemployment, our misuse of our environment. John Westerhoff, in *A Pilgrim People* and other books, demonstrates in a challenging way that the cycle of the Church's Year can be employed to show how God's story of his life and action among us and in his creation intersects with our stories as they unfold in the course of our life pilgrimage.

The kaleidoscopic changes and shifts of mood, need and pace, of desire, expectation and possibility in our lives strike responses in God's as his story is told by the Church. We move with God up to mountain peaks of Resurrection awareness and fall into the depths of our despair and blindness, to be lifted by him again into his light; but we also travel with him through periods of 'ordinary time' when we can re-examine, refurbish or readjust our equipment of pilgrimage. We move from celebration to commitment, from deepening commitment to deepening joy as '...in living the faithful life we come to faith...'.[1] Our lives, with all their problems as well as all their joys, become illumined and nurtured by his life as together we progress along the Way. We can find a place to share the experiences of our pilgrimage in all-age Activity Days, when they are so planned that they relate an aspect of the Church's Year to a particular theme from life.

An example of how the Church's story might be seen to intersect with our stories through an activity day or event might be the planning of a Pentecost event in which the gifts of the Spirit are celebrated and explored. The empowering of ordinary men and women to become the Church says something about what God intends for us all: the fulfilment of our potential and the realisation of our personhood. Certainly this example is rich in possibilities: one might be to show what, in our contemporary situation, assaults human dignity and prevents people from realising their potential. Unemployment, homelessness, issues of health and education, drug,

29

tobacco or alcohol abuse, exploitative advertising: here is an opportunity to bring to matters of basic importance the illumination afforded by the Gospel story and the Church's experience.

If it is planned to do this activity, then it is important to build into the day a point at which to consider how to deepen the effectiveness of your church's ministry of care and involvement. For example, could Christian people be encouraged to support the efforts to face these problems that already exist in their community? Perhaps such an event could begin to show what kinds of initiative a local church might take and how the potential for ministry to be found in people of all ages could best be used. It might be as straightforward as knitting fingerless gloves for the local elderly to help against the winter cold, or as major a step as working together to provide a place of welcome and care for the homeless or unemployed.

Another example of how the Church's story can be shown to intersect with our stories, those of our community and the world in which we live, might be a Rogationtide 'workshop' activity day or weekend. We explore God's Creation, given into our hands. We examine the gifts we have been given, to create from their materials our own 'creations' to eat and enjoy; through the help of our children as we work together we return to a sense of wonder and delight in Creation's delicate patterns of relationship and beauty; through our heightened awareness of it, we realise with sorrow our abuse of all that is implied by the phrase 'the land'.

Workshops to explore the local environment against the background of scriptural insight (it is amazing what an urban environment will reveal), workshops to celebrate the gifts we have of using for pleasure and sustenance the materials of God's Creation, workshops to explore how we can begin to be more deeply aware of our responsibility to care for our created world (one such 'workshop' involved a trip to a local beach, where young and old after a 'clean-up' created a 'trashman' from cans and bits of flotsam, to be presented as an act of penitence at the Sunday Eucharist): such exploration has its own particular power in bringing us into sensitive touch with God's Life within, among and around us. Indeed, it has been said that the delicate health of our spiritual relationships, factors which make up 'person', depend upon how these reflect and are informed by the fragile and intricate balances that are nature and the land.[2] It is because this relationship between person and land has been so distorted and broken that we are in the grip of a spiritual and physical

30

malaise threatening our own destruction and that of our planet home.
The following diagram shows the stages of an event seen as a whole,
from inception, through reflection to further action.

ROGATIONTIDE EVENT

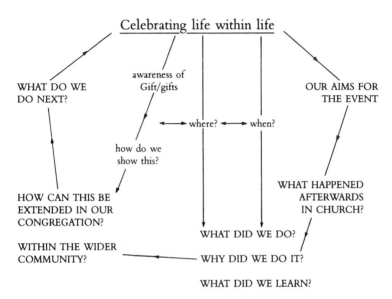

Celebrating life within life

WHAT DO WE
DO NEXT?

awareness of
Gift/gifts

OUR AIMS FOR
THE EVENT

where? ← → when?

how do we
show this?

WHAT HAPPENED
AFTERWARDS
IN CHURCH?

HOW CAN THIS BE
EXTENDED IN OUR
CONGREGATION?

WITHIN THE WIDER
COMMUNITY?

WHAT DID WE DO?

WHY DID WE DO IT?

WHAT DID WE LEARN?

Such events can be a marvellous opportunity for a church not only
to become aware how the story of Faith relates to and is illumined by
the life of the local community, but also to reach out and learn from
the skills of folk in the community who may appear to have no obvious
connection with 'church' at all. The pigeon-fancier, the agnostic
woodcarver, the electronics engineer, the embroiderer – what a
wonderful means of recognising the story of the community while
living God's story together, but in the welcoming and enabling
warmth of his love. A celebration of the skills, the experience and
culture of the neighbourhood from which a congregation is drawn
should, ideally, include insights from other religions and attitudes.
Dare we do that?

> 'I've just come from a long and dispirited PCC meeting
> where the sole topic of debate was our impossible financial
> situation. Trust? Mutual regard? Tolerance? Sadly, such a

31

spirit was not evident; only a rancorous bickering over money. How can we ever hope to do any of this "getting together" with all the congregation in order to learn and grow together if a few of us can't even work together on mutual concerns?'

Realities can be so hard that the best hopes and intentions are crushed by them. A congregation fighting, with meagre resources, a losing battle to save decaying buildings and to ensure its own survival can become trapped in a cycle of despair, the very antithesis of Christian joy and hope. Parishes and congregations, like the individuals they are called to serve, can themselves become the victims of isolation and loneliness.

Perhaps a first step to help themselves might be to have a very informal PCC meeting with an open invitation to others interested, held somewhere other than the regular venue. (One small parish utilised the local pub for this purpose.) It would be made very clear from the start that the only purpose of meeting should be to think about and discuss practical ideas for encouraging an 'all-age' strategy of approach to the congregation's own life and its ministry of outreach to the community. A small group might be formed with the purpose of bringing consistent thought and prayer to the need, and of keeping it as a priority of concern before the congregation. In larger parishes where resources pose less of a problem and there may be a working committee structure, even including a 'parish education committee', a small 'all-age' group with the purpose of viewing congregational life and ministry from that perspective could still be very useful.

Despite its diocesan and deanery structure, the Church of England shows little evidence of the co-operative, sharing spirit of life and ministry in which different elements support and enable one another. The spirit of determined pride in individual identity too often isolates parishes and congregations from one another. Perhaps groups of parishes could begin to think and plan together. The Deanery, if not too large, could also be a support. Certainly each Deanery could have an 'all-age' planning group of its own.

Chapter 6 of this book will help with suggestions for activities with various aims within this broad area. Activity Days, Deanery or Parish Pilgrimages, Deanery or Parish Group Fun Days...the local circumstances, properly explored, will yield their own ideas. In one deanery an 'all-age' Quest Day, which involved journeying to neighbouring places of worship armed with clue sheets and search games, culminating in a barbecue and simple act of worship, provided one meeting point for the parishioners from different parishes. If such days are to be significantly more than an enjoyable outing, however, they will need to include at some point an opportunity for thoughtful reflection together sharing...perhaps over a spare rib and Coke. They must be seen as parts of a process of deepened commitment to the kind of shared learning and experiencing which 'all-age' is all about.

Various experiences in different Churches – for these are already a rich resource among us to be shared – say a great deal about the spirit of an 'all-age' approach to our life and living as a Church. The story of our Faith and of God's action among and through us, as it is told through the cycle of the Church's Year, can come to fresh life for us as it explains and enriches our own life story. It can also enlighten our own story, by giving it God's intended value. Then we are free to unfold within the riches of God's grace while, with our own inherent value, enriching the stories of others. Children and adults, young and old, all sorts and conditions, enriching and learning from one another's stories in the light of God's Story lived among and for us: this is the pilgrim road of God's people – together.

SUMMARY OF IDEAS FOR LEARNING TOGETHER
Fun Days
This chapter starts with a fun day. For many parishes this is the beginning of all-age activity. It should not be the end!
What sort of day should it be?

Try: a Sports Day – with a range of sporting activities. Go together to a skittle alley, ice rink, swimming pool, table-tennis hall. If some don't wish to participate, they could be encouraged to draw, write up, comment on tape on the activities, to share later at a tea or supper, barbecue, camp fire.

Try: a Parish Plod – a walk together round the boundaries of the parish, to a place of pilgrimage, to a local beauty spot. Some groups have done this pushing members in wheel-chairs and prams.

Try: an afternoon or evening of Victorian entertainment, songs, music hall, recitations – or medieval, or any other period.

Try: a 'Generation Game' evening – Trivial Pursuit, Beetle Drive, cards. Give time for refreshments and chat, organise teams for team games.

Try: a Saint's Day Soiree, Pancake Party, Pentecost Party, Epiphany Event. We *need* to use the festivals we have for *celebration* and enjoyment together.

Notes
1. *A Pilgrim People*, John H. Westerhoff (Harper and Row).
2. *Crossing Open Ground*, Barry Lopez (Picador: Pan Books).

5. Signs of the Kingdom

'Dear Dorothy,

Our Church has been struggling for some years now to work through the implications of what it means to have a fully integrated church community; in terms of worship, learning and service. I do hope that some of our experiences will be of encouragement to your readers who are moving in the same direction.

It all began with a new vicar, as many things do in the Church of England! He suggested that the PCC and other leaders within the church should get together to formulate a Parish Plan, taking into consideration the various aspects of our organisation – buildings, mission and evangelism, stewardship, education and training, pastoral, worship and decision making. We had to consider the purpose of each aspect, the aims and objectives we needed to achieve with a time scale. We had never been so organised! It was our normal practice to drift along from week to week, keeping to tradition and changing as little as possible, and so it came as somewhat of a shock when we began to look for signs of the Kingdom in our church life. As we began to share together our hopes and dreams of how we, as God's People, should be living as members of his Kingdom, we began to realise the urgency of the task and how we needed to work together, young and old, to make the vision a reality.

We had very little experience of sharing, learning and working together across the age groups, and so we spent the first year in fellowship together before our main service on Sunday mornings – sharing our thoughts on the theme and its relevance to the way we live, and gathering our prayers and concerns together to offer at the Eucharist. Every person, whatever their age, was valued and their contribution was accepted by the other members of the congregation.

This weekly activity became the school where we learnt what it means to be the Pilgrim Church. It was important for us equally to love and accept those people who felt unable to take part in this new way of celebrating the liturgy, so they became partners with us as the traditional pattern of the Eucharist unfolded. They, at the same time, accepted the new ways of reflecting on God's word and intercession. What was offered as an experiment for a year is now a regular feature of our corporate life together as we meet for worship week by week. People meet during the week in their different age groups and to pursue a variety of interests, but for children and adults alike the highlight of our corporate Christian lives is the time we spend together on Sunday mornings.

As the years have gone on we have seen the objectives of our Parish Plan be fulfilled and new ones developed – each has become a sign of our spiritual growth and the Kingdom of God in the midst of us.'

It is hoped that this book has already given some encouragement to its readers to adapt the traditional and try something new. Occasional all-age learning or worship events, however, whilst being very effective tasters, are not sufficient in themselves to develop the sense of corporate pilgrimage which lies at the very heart of Christianity.

'Christianity is a process of being and becoming, a way of listening and hearing, a way of responding and a way of living in the light of the clues along the way, the meaning and the purpose of life given in Jesus Christ. The Christian has never arrived; always there is the potential of growth.'

(*Learning Community*, John Sutcliffe)

As the all-age experience becomes part of the ongoing life of the local Christian community, as the faith stories of the past and present are shared, new strategies for the way we conduct every aspect of our corporate life should emerge and a clear all-age parish policy develop. Suggestions for such a policy and programme are developed in Chapter 6, page 41.

The decision-making body within the local church (for Anglicans, the Parochial Church Council) needs to become aware of the needs, talents and ministries of all people within the congregation, and these must be reflected in their discussions. Whatever is on the agenda – whether it is a new altar frontal, a programme for the year's activities or the annual budget – all these should be considered in the light of how they will affect the faith development of people of all ages. The resulting decision would almost inevitably release individuals for service in some way which would, in turn, become a sign of the Kingdom. In all our concerns the question should be not only 'how does this affect people of all ages, both those committed to the Faith and those who hold no such conviction?' but also 'how can people of different ages be set free to minister both *to one another* and *with one another* in the world?' Enabling a PCC and a congregation to reach this point is a task that needs all the support, encouragement and expertise available in the diocese, deanery and parish.

The effectiveness of a parish's decision-making body will rely heavily on whether its members have been given the time and opportunity to reflect prayerfully on the matters in hand with a small group representing all ages. This could happen naturally if the worship pattern explained in the letter at the beginning of this chapter were adopted. In this context we see that all-age learning, worship and living cannot be separated – yet so often in our church education programmes there is a reluctance to provide opportunities for all ages to learn together, even though it has yet to be demonstrated that adults learn and perceive in ways which are decisively different from those ways in which children learn. Everything that is important in the learning situation and process for the child is important for the adult. The generalisation that a person notices twenty per cent of what he hears, thirty per cent of what he sees, fifty per cent of what he both hears and sees, seventy per cent of what he himself says and ninety per cent of what he himself does is true, irrespective of the age of the person.

It is therefore necessary to ask whether separate learning activities for adults and children are always appropriate. There may be occasions when people learn in their particular age or interest groups, but these 'learnings' need to be reflected and shared with the whole congregation. The most natural way of learning, however, in a church where all-age principles are being worked out is to provide the opportunity, for example in Lent groups, for people of all ages to learn together. We are not helped in this matter by national organisations such as the British Council of Churches, who take major initiatives in the inter-church process without giving due and careful consideration to the needs of all members. They neglect to provide suitable material and direct advice to group leaders on how to incorporate the younger people into the study programme (whether it be by having groups of mixed ages as well as denominations, or by convening children's groups and sharing together at the end of the course). Much disservice is done to ecumenism by an unwillingness to include the young in discussions. Another question which will arise as a result of this is the impact, or lack of it, of the Week of Prayer for Christian Unity on the young.

It is often suggested that there are aspects of the Christian Faith which are beyond the reach of a person because of their lack of cognitive development, and at every age this may be true. Understanding may also be limited by *experience* but, particularly in matters of faith, this bears very little relationship to the *age* of a person. Neither limitation should be a determining, controlling factor in all-age activities and learning. All people need to be given the opportunity to think and share their understanding and belief, not only with others from their own church, churchmanship and denomination; they also need, from time to time, the chance to engage with the richness of traditions which are not their own.

The Church needs to take the task of education far more seriously and encourage its people to take full responsibility for their ongoing learning and spiritual growth. Faith stories are not the property of individuals. They should be set alongside those of our forefathers, Abraham, Isaac and Jacob, and thus become a corporate learning experience for the Christian community. A serious commitment to continuous reflected learning through experience across the age groups will eliminate the need for the kind of formal 'taught' courses we have at the present time for (for example) Confirmation preparation.

Whenever the education programme of the Church is under review (and it should be, constantly) the questions to be addressed are:

What indications do we have that individual learning has taken place?

What effect has this learning had on the lives of the individuals and how they conduct themselves?

What effect has this individual learning had on the Christian community and, as a result, what is the next step we have to take in our corporate pilgrimage?

The local Christian community is the shop window for the Kingdom of God down our street. If passers-by see the same display week after week, month after month and year after year, covered in cobwebs and a thick layer of dust, they are hardly likely to be attracted. If, however, the display is altered week by week according to the new gifts discovered and offered by the owners, this – combined with an ever-open door, through which can be seen the ongoing work of providing the very best service to customers – will be a far more attractive proposition.

We come back once more to local management, or the PCC, and the stewardship of resources. This in itself is an educative process and should be shared between old and young alike. For as long as the Baptism rite contains the words, 'We are members together of the Body of Christ', all need to grow in their understanding of what that belonging means in terms of responsibilities, both in respect of resourcing the local Christian community, and also those services provided by the diocese and the national Church. The proportion of time, talents and finance which is to be allotted to evangelism, mission and relief agencies must also be considered. Under our present structures, all these areas have an intrinsic value in the development of the Kingdom; it is important for children as they grow, as well as adults, to own them and to work out their stewardship in that context. Again, this can only be done if knowledge and experience is shared between members.

Just one small example of a project which has become, in some churches, an all-age activity is where the work of Christian Aid is a matter of common concern. As Christian Aid Week approaches each year people of all ages come together to think and pray about the current issues highlighted by the Agency. They then go out in twos, adult and child, to do the door-to-door collecting. What once may have been a chore becomes a learning experience, a deepening of faith through greater understanding and reflection, and an informed opinion which becomes an act of witness to the world.

There are so many ways in which adults and children can be set free for ministry to one another and to the world. One of the most powerful signs of the Kingdom is the Church's ministry among the sick, the lonely and the bereaved. In a Church that understands the value of sharing concerns and prayer between its members, whatever their age, it would be quite natural for this to be reflected in the pastoral team. How fruitful it would be if, where appropriate, each adult visitor could be accompanied by a child, both of them holding in common the understanding that Jesus heals the sick and loves the lonely and sad.

Perhaps there is a call here for Christians to break down the barriers of suspicion which naturally prevail in almost any group of people. Suspicion makes us fear and fail to trust the joint insights, wisdom and actions of such a group. The Christian community of all ages is not such a group. It is, rather, a community of people who are vitally related to one another, people so vitally inter-related that their very fate is in the hands of the others in the community. This is the community of faith: a eucharistic community, a community under the guidance of the Holy Spirit through Baptism, a community with a common mission to the world. Its members have no need to fear the outcome of such a gathering, whether it be in terms of shared liturgy, learning or service to mankind.

SUMMARY OF IDEAS FOR LEARNING TOGETHER
This chapter reflects on the results of all-age learning in a particular parish.
Some of the letters in Chapter 6 add further valuable comments and reflection on what it has meant to people to be in a parish where all ages worship and learn together.

6. Further Ideas, Examples and Reactions

'Dear Dorothy,

As a priest one is constantly having to live with the expectations that others have of you and sometimes it is extremely difficult to try and keep up appearances.

The other Sunday was a particularly bad day. The week had had several pressures, and there had been several difficult meetings with people. Various people had let others down. I'd had several arguments and they'd been unresolved...and now I had to stand behind the altar and celebrate the Eucharist.

I was in a right state... Nobody loved me...the world was a terrible mess...why should I have to come to church when others didn't?

I thought that perhaps the liturgy might help, but I'm afraid it didn't. The Confession just made things worse. Thank goodness lay people were reading the lessons and leading the intercessions. I managed to control myself during the sermon, relying heavily on some theatrical experience. Outwardly little was noticeable, but inwardly I was sending positive hate waves out to everybody...

The collection was taken and the bread and wine offered and my mood became darker and blacker.

The choir sang the Sanctus, "Holy, Holy Lord..."

In the silence that followed, a small toddler from the back

of the church started to mimic the choir and "Holy loly laly holy laly loly..." echoed around the church.

It broke the wicked spell, the hate disappeared and I was able to join the company of earth and heaven.

I inwardly thanked God for that toddler who by simply being himself had opened up the gate of heaven for me. Thank God also that mum and dad hadn't stopped him. The choir giggled, members of the congregation sitting around were smiling, and, thank God, so was I.'

'Dear Dorothy,

I recently helped at an All-Age Day and one of the comments made by a teenager during the event made a great impact on me.

After the Sunday morning service about 30 people moved into the local church school for a shared picnic lunch, followed by activities exploring the theme of Reconciliation. The sermon and lessons had already explored this during a communion service. People of all ages were able to choose from a wide range of activities including painting. The teenager I mentioned at the beginning chose to explore painting. She was an extremely clever girl, academically brilliant, and had been promised an almost unconditional place at University.

Towards the end of the day we asked people to share what they had done and what the experience meant to them. When it came to her turn she admitted some initial reserve about the idea, as she was used to using her brain and liked to have intellectual discussions. She said that the painting experience had showed her that there was another side to her brain and that "It was wonderful to use that part of me that wasn't dependent upon logical thoughts and arguments. It has been a very pleasant change to writing A level essays."

I valued this comment greatly as it said something to me about the integration of ourselves, a sort of healing, indeed an aspect of reconciliation. This girl had given herself and me a glimpse of our spiritual pilgrimage.'

'Dear Dorothy,

At a recent Saturday Lent course in the diocese we had as our subject "Icons and Spirituality". Children and adults were invited and a few of the adults offered to help the children's group paint icons. The rest of the adults had a visiting artist and he was to talk about his work as an icon painter.

Those of us in the children's group painted on blocks of wood, mixed the powder paint with an egg yolk and decorated our pictures with gold leaf, paint and sequins. We learned that an icon is a vision of heaven and that the block of wood is separated into heaven and earth. This is done by carving a border around the wood, leaving a central space in which the picture is painted.

We all took a great deal of time and care thinking about the subject matter and many of us spent a considerable amount of time in silence thinking of our favourite Bible story or life of a saint. There followed a quiet air of industry as, with great care, we started the painting of our icons. This was true of the youngest who was four years old and the oldest who was 40.

Before we showed the rest of the group our finished works of art we spent thirty minutes deciding in which order they should go. The discussion that followed was one of those times of illumination and a glimpse of the holy. It went something like this...

"Whose picture should go first?"

"Well, Alice's should." (Alice was the four-year-old) "She's at the beginning of her life so hers should go first."

"Yes that's right...anyway her picture looks like the beginning of the world." (It was a typical four-year-old painting, splodges with little sequins stuck all over it.) "It's like space."

"Do you know what's underneath all that?"

"No...what?"

"She drew a picture of Jesus first. He's got all covered up...he's underneath it all!"

"Mine should go next...it's Noah's Ark and the rainbow,

it's about a new beginning...things starting all over again."

After some silence:

"My picture of Mary and the Angel Gabriel must come next."

"Why?"

"Well, Jesus is safe in the ark of Mary's tummy."

"My picture of the baby Jesus and Mary is next. That's what happens in the story...and it's about a new creation..."

"This picture is of Jesus as a man, it's after his baptism, he's coming up out of the water."

"Oh, that's like creation...that came out of the water."

"Yes and babies are in water in their mummy's tummy."

"I've done a picture of Jesus on the cross..."

A silence followed...and I just needed some time to take in all this information.

The picture of Jesus painted in white and gold followed, representing the Risen Christ, and finally a picture of St Catherine symbolised the lives of saints as they make the cross and tomb their own. We were in a fairly dark room and the electric light shining on the sequins and gold paint made the icons vibrant and alive.

"We must have a blank piece of wood at the end," said one of the children.

"Why is that?"

"So that all the others can put their own pictures on to it."

"Yes...so that it goes on forever.."

The time came for us to enter the room with the other adults. One of the children shared our insights with them.

"We've spent a great deal of time talking about icons," said one of the adults, "but you have just shown us what they are about."

"I wished I had come and done the painting," said another.

"What you have just shared with us has complemented our

discussions," said another.

"Could we borrow your pictures and put them up in the centre?"

The looks on the children's faces said it all...their icons were far too precious. We politely declined and said that we wanted to take them home, for we understood that an icon came to greater life in the quietness of a darkened room lit by candle-light.

Several comments came back the following week that this had indeed happened.'

'Dear Dorothy,

Have you heard of parachute games? Well I hadn't until a few weeks ago. A young youth worker came to our Parish Weekend and taught us how to play them. I must admit that I was rather suspicious at first. There were about twenty of us there; the youngest was three years old, the oldest 65. Well...we all had to stand around the edge of an old parachute that was stretched out on the grass. This young youth leader then told us to take the edges of the parachute and gently waft it in the air, then on the count of three we all had to throw it up as high as we could and still hold on. She called it "making a mushroom"...quite a good name, I thought. Everybody was laughing and after my initial hesitation I must admit that I had the occasional smile as well. Anyway, we played quite a few other games and the young children seemed to be enjoying themselves a lot. I was just getting into the swing of things when our young leader told us that for the next game we were to take turns and lie down in the middle of the parachute and on the count of three everybody would lift it up and support us...My heart started to beat, I can tell you...She did say that we didn't have to do it if we didn't want to...but nobody seemed to be dropping out. I wasn't dressed for this for a start and the first thought that went through my head was, "They'll drop me," and I couldn't bear that...

However I found myself lying in the centre...How I got there I'll never know. I tucked my skirt in between my legs and almost every muscle became tense. There was the count of three and then suddenly...

Well, all I can say is that it was like a vision. It didn't last long, probably only for a split second. It was as if time had slowed down. I was gently raised from the ground and gently rocked to and fro. As I lay there I saw a parable, a vision. I don't know what the right word is, but I felt supported and upheld by God. I had the briefest of insights of what I think God is like. Then I saw that the parachute and the game was a parable of what the church should be like. Everybody was holding and supporting me, even the smallest child...They were showing what God is like...

That was three weeks ago and I am grateful for that game and what it taught me.

PS I was the 65-year-old...next time I shall wear trousers.'

'Dear Dorothy,

Do you remember the letter I wrote about my son in Chartres Cathedral? Well, it reminds me of the occasions when we reached Lourdes. During the evening thousands of pilgrims join in a torchlight procession. Everybody has a candle and sings choruses. The children decided that they would like to join in. I think that the idea of carrying a lighted candle and singing repetitive choruses appealed to them. We found ourselves in about the middle of the procession and there was one point, halfway around, when we could see all the thousands of people in front of us and all the thousands behind. My five-year-old's mouth dropped and then he exclaimed loudly,

"Cor!!! ALL these people believe in Jesus and God..."

He had caught a glimpse of the Church Militant here on earth. Here was a visible symbol of the saints of God carrying their lights in the world.

Both these experiences and others have melted some of my stupid religious prejudices...'

'Dear Dorothy,

The church to which I belong is part of a Team Ministry and once a year the churches in the Team combine for their main Sunday morning Eucharist. I would like to share with you what happened this year. It was with some apprehension that I agreed to accompany my friend because the service was to be held in St Mary's and I had heard that they do it differently there. The arthritis in my hands and failing sight make it difficult for me to follow a different order of service in a strange book.

Well...some parts of the service were different to what I am used to but we were gently taken through it by the nice young Team Vicar with the aid of a booklet. The best part for me was during the time for intercession when we were all given a cut-out figure which represented ourselves and we were invited to offer our own prayers either by writing or drawing them on the figures. Then when we came up to the altar rails to receive Communion we brought our prayers with us and placed them in the sanctuary.

For the first time in my life I had been asked to share something of myself in worship and it was a moving experience to see my figure lying next to many others, belonging to both adults and the children, all of us, with our hopes, dreams and thanksgivings, placed there at the feet of Jesus.'

'Dear Dorothy,

My little girl, aged seven, asked me to come with her to the Sunday school party. At our church this is rather special as it does not take the form of a traditional party with jellies, balloons and children's entertainment. Rather it happens on the afternoon of Palm Sunday and the whole congregation as well as parents are invited to take part.

We began the celebration by being asked to imagine what it must have been like living in Palestine as a follower of Jesus during the week which led up to his death; our thoughts were helped along the way by the use of some slides. We then divided up into groups of mixed ages; my daughter decided to stay with me, to look at different events which occurred during the final week of our Lord's life and their implications for us today. After a shared tea we then presented our thoughts to the other groups either visually or through the spoken word in an act of worship. Our group looked at Good Friday and as part of our thinking together my daughter and I rubbed a tile in the church which depicted the symbols of the crucifixion, the cross, the dice, the spear and the seamless robe. Normally I find it quite difficult to talk to my family about Christian things but as we were rubbing the tile together my daughter began with the question, "What were the dice for, Mummy?" and we spoke together, at great depth, about Jesus and his great love for us.

How I wish the church would create more opportunities such as the one I have outlined above where parents can share and learn alongside their children. These experiences can then be taken back into our homes, treasured and used in our daily life.'

'Dear Dorothy,

I was somewhat alarmed when the vicar told me at our monthly churchwardens' meeting that next Sunday, instead of the sermon during the morning service, we would be doing a Bible study in church. To my mind, studying the Bible is something you do at home or in a house group, definitely not during the Eucharist on a Sunday morning, especially when children are present.

However, he was unmoved by my protestations and so the Bible study went ahead as planned and, to my utter amazement, became a growth point in the life of our church and brought about a great change in my own attitudes.

We looked at the Bible story of Jesus going to the temple with his parents when he was twelve years old. The vicar introduced the story – he told it simply, giving some background information. We were then divided up into mixed age groups and were asked to look at the story from the point of view of the different characters in it: what made them think and behave in a certain way. Our group took the character of Jesus and, as it happened, there was a young boy of about twelve years of age in our group. The cynics amongst us could not help wondering why the boy Jesus had not shown some thoughtfulness towards his parents by informing them of his intention to remain in the temple. The boy in our group, in answer to this, related the time when he went sailing with a friend. The weather was warm and sunny and the wind was just right. As the sails of the yacht caught the wind they sped through the water and time stood still. They were caught up in the experience of the moment and it wasn't until they reached shore that they discovered that "two hours' sailing" had taken up most of the day. Of course they found worried parents at home. I think it was the experience of this young lad that made me realise that when we are about the Father's business, whether it is in prayer or service, we too can allow time to stand still and he becomes the priority.

At the end of the study, when we shared our learning with members of the other groups, I was conscious that for many of us there had been a renewed commitment to spend more time with God, listening to what he has to say to us and sharing our experience of faith with one another. Needless to say we now don't mind too much if our worship and learning together takes up a bit more of our time on Sunday mornings!'

'Dear Dorothy,

Please do not be offended by what I am about to say in this letter about your recent visit to our parish.

I must admit that I took umbrage at the suggestion, implied by your visit and that irritating video "Children in the Way", that we are not doing enough for our children. We have a thriving Junior Church (33 members) and a very large Pathfinders group. These each have their own services every Sunday and church-people are therefore able to worship with dignity and in peace in the manner appropriate to them. In our church all ages (to use what appears to be fast becoming a tired cliché) are therefore catered to. This 'All-Age Worship' talk seems simply to mean a superficial watering down of the Bible truths taught by Jesus. Not all of us need "milk suitable for babies". I am a "born again Christian" and I need solid meat, this is impossible if we are going to have to accommodate children

Sunday by Sunday. Children need to be *taught* before they can properly read the road signs along the way, the Gospel of *The Great Teacher!'*

'Dear Dorothy,

About four years ago the children in church used to begin the service with the adults and leave halfway through the service to go into Junior Church. They went home immediately after Junior Church finished. In a church meeting it was mentioned that this felt wrong, especially as they were not in church for the Communion service and the whole meaning of the Communion service was to bring the whole church together. The children then began to leave for the first part of the service and return to join the circle of communicants. We had touched on an important principle which led us to look deeper into the role of children. If we, as a congregation, felt it important that the whole family of the church should come together, then why should we bring them in only so far and exclude them from the sacraments?

In our church, after the minister has blessed the sacraments, we stand in a circle and pass the sacraments to each other. Being an LEP we have many people from different religious backgrounds, all of whom at that time had their own ideas about whether children should or should not receive them.

I remember my own experience in this situation. At that time my children were 2 and 5 years old. I remember Rebecca holding her hands out for the bread and I could no longer refuse to give it to her because I felt it would have been confining the grace of God and what right had I to do that. Before joining the LEP, I had a C of E background where it was usual for children to receive the sacraments only after being confirmed but, looking on my daughter's face, I had no hesitation in feeling I had done the right thing. Problems occurred, however, when I sensed across the circle a sense of uneasiness, especially from the older members of the congregation and I wondered if I had the right to make them feel so uneasy and I was very much aware of their feelings.

I was not the only mother in the Communion circle going through this experience. With the other mothers we felt a sensitivity toward the other communicants but at the same time we found it difficult to believe that God confines children.

During this period of being aware of both the rest of the congregation and my children, on a few occasions I did not give my children the sacraments, being aware who was in the circle and how it would make them feel, but as I continued in that way I slowly began to feel very heavy and torn and soon didn't look forward to facing this situation every second Sunday morning. The worst thing happened when one Sunday morning I refused my children the sacraments. I remember Rebecca, my oldest child, being very upset and asking me "Why?" and for a long time after that she refused to join the circle.

Luckily our ministers recognised the pain in the situation and decided to face the issue head-on. For three weeks running we gave over the Sunday morning worship to discussing it. As a congregation together we searched the gospels. What would Jesus do? Not only did we search the gospels but we listened to the children. We couldn't get past the phrase "Suffer little children to come unto me and forbid them not, for such is the kingdom of heaven".

Children listened to adults and adults listened to children, and we were all openly honest. We told each other of our upbringings and of our traditions. Children talked openly how sometimes they felt the adults were happier when they were in Junior Church so they couldn't be disturbed. Adults talked of how noise affected their hearing aids. In between honest down-to-earth comments, both negative and positive, over a period of weeks, we were realising that we were just getting to know each other and maybe there appeared just an inkling of love.

This whole experience changed us. Today we find it very easy to accept the children taking the sacraments. We had to go through some pain but it was worth it because in that circle we are not strangers but we are truly a loving family. We continue to listen and learn from our children. One typical comment comes to mind when I realise the wisdom children have. A young nine-year-old got very angry after studying the Lord's Prayer. "If God is supposed to give us our daily bread, why do we have to kill the animals?" And in another lesson, "If Jesus turned over the tables in the temple, why do we sell things on stalls during St Mark's tide?"

Jesus said, "Unless you become like one of these children, you cannot enter the kingdom of heaven".'

'Dear Dorothy,

I have attended other churches but not felt the warmth and friendliness with both young and old as I do at St Mark's. We sit in a circle, in some parts two deep, in others three or four deep, but all the faces are visible. I am not looking at the back of someone's head, wondering who is it?

Both young and old take Communion together. We often join hands for a few moments before we start, with children giving and receiving from adults and vice versa – it is a pleasure to watch and receive. When it is finished and we give our thanks, the feeling of being together is still there as we move back to our chairs. Our children at St Mark's have views about things that happen and they are listened to and encouraged just the same as adults – after all, they are the adults of the future of St Mark's.'

'Dear Dorothy,

Our children join in our service at the point where we share the Peace and they are welcomed into the Communion circle to share the celebration with us. When we first started this practice there was some resentment from older members which the children recognised. They reacted by feeling and looking uncomfortable and sometimes with adverse behaviour. But now, after talking this matter through with all concerned, there is a greater understanding and caring among both young and old members and the children are very comfortable during the celebration. This reflects in their relaxed attitude and the joy that is shown when they are serving an adult with bread and wine.'

'Dear Dorothy,

One of the nice things about St Mark's is the way the children are accepted by the rest of the congregation as they are, and now are also accepted in the Communion. Although it has taken a long time for the children to be accepted in the Communion, they now take an active role and feel they belong to the Church completely.

No-one is pressurised into taking Communion but it's there if they want it. At first many adults thought that the children would not be able to understand the meaning of Communion, but if you ask them about it they all know it's about Christ and sharing love. In fact, some of the children's views have given some adults a new perspective on Communion.

Another good thing about St Mark's is all the congregation get on well with each other and there are no small groups who talk about people. Everyone will help if they can and all new members are warmly welcomed.

Many people like the format of the church service as it allows the children to come in halfway through the service and join in. This means they do not get bored as they are not in for the whole service, but they do not feel they are not included as they go in later.

Nearly all the children enjoy coming to church and they all feel as if they are included as equals. I was nine years old when I came to St Mark's and I have always enjoyed being there. Although my Mam would not allow me to have Communion before I was confirmed, I felt the atmosphere was a lot freer, as children could have Communion and I didn't feel as if being a child made me a lot different. Although it was strange joining an Ecumenical Church, which met in a school, I now wouldn't want to change it for anything else.'

'Dear Dorothy,

I like the idea of our Sunday school coming into the church halfway through the service. In my old church the Sunday school was in a totally separate building and we didn't always come into the church. Coming into the service makes children still feel part of the adults' service. The Sunday school teachers can also be a part of the service instead of having to stay out with the children all the time.

The part in the service where sometimes Rob reads a children's book is different. I don't think it should always be a part of the service but all of the stories have morals and are fun so it gets a point over well.

Communion is strange to me. I don't believe children should take Communion until they are confirmed. This may be because I couldn't take Communion until I was confirmed. I don't think that (whatever the parents or children say) they really understand why they are taking the Communion until they follow the course. This shouldn't really be a bad thing because I thought I was given a special kind of peace with the vicar's hand on my head. This is something adults don't get and was special. I don't think children should take bread and drink wine because they taste nice and adults do it.'

'Dear Dorothy,
I have read many books on Christianity and Love, but it took the children of St Mark's to give me a deeper understanding.

I am a Sunday school teacher at St Mark's, but it is usually the children who teach me.

Some of the youngest of the children take Communion even before Confirmation. I don't feel it wrong of them. "Who are we to say that they shouldn't because they're too young to understand the sacramental reason of the Body and Blood of Christ?" "Who are we to say how the mind of a child works?" Some Churches have a ruling that children must be confirmed before they take Communion. "Why?" If a child has been baptised in church and continues his/her worship there, surely his/her growth in body, mind and spirit is his/her confirmation. His/her growth within the fellowship of the Church is their confirmation. Confirmation is a man-made rule. "Was it Christ's also?" "Would he turn a child away because they weren't confirmed?"

We have a child member on the Parish Church Council.

"Why not?" They have a right also in the running of the church, etc.

The children enjoy their work in Sunday school and enjoy sharing their work and stories with the adults.

Some things the children say make me laugh/happy.'

'Dear Dorothy,
"Don't let my children go!"
As I travel around the diocese in my job as Children's Adviser I often long to misquote Exodus as above! Sometimes the children appear for a few minutes or are taken off to Sunday school, where excellent work is often being done – but they do not reappear in church. It is not surprising, is it, that we then lose them when they reach an age when Sunday school seems irrelevant for them and they leave? They've never felt or been a real part of the worshipping congregation, so see no need or incentive to be so at the age of 11-12-13 or whatever.

In some churches the children do not come to the church at all, but go directly to Sunday school, club or something similar.

There are parishes, however, where the children are very much part of the gathered congregation. They come in at some significant point such as the "Peace", and share in a meaningful way in what is happening. In other churches children remain for the entire service and their worship is a part of the programme in which learning also takes place at a separate time for everyone – in groups later on Sunday or in the week.

The parishes which are experimenting with having children present for the entire worship, and are thinking out ideas for all ages to worship and learn together in various ways, are discovering the sober truth that to exclude the young is actually to impoverish our own worship and growth in faith.

Having children in church is not an invitation for chaos, noise, toddler feet pounding up and down the aisle, or for everything to be "diluted" so that children can understand.

Surely part of our Christian witness and commitment is to help the young to realise how and why and when worship contains silence, times when we stand, sit, more quietly, consider others, etc. Children are capable of great depths of spiritual understanding and respond to times in worship that enable them to experience awe, wonder, mystery, love, colour, light and joy. We impoverish our children's faith if we assume that they cannot and will not sit still for a time, join in, share with us.

Our worship must be attractive, it must be apparent that it is significant and meaningful to us. If we adults appear bored and uninterested, restless and critical, then children will respond to our attitudes. If they see it as something we go to joyfully with expectation, and our expectations are met by the endless possibilities of new things happening, new ideas in the context of familiar liturgy, then we are blessed indeed, for our children will not "go" but remain to share with us their vitality, their discoveries, their growth, their faith as all ages worship and learn together.'

Worship On The Edge: a true experience

Two families gathered on a lonely stretch of Welsh sand. They heaped up a miniature sand-altar and stuck on it a cross put together from driftwood; then gathered round it in a huddle, the leader upwind of the tight-knit human horseshoe. There was silence except for the plashing of waves and the flapping of a Force Five breeze.

'The Lord is here,' said the leader, and back came the response, challenging the wind. Then followed a home-made Benedicite...'You wheeling gulls, bless the Lord...Praise him and magnify him for ever. You foaming waves, bless the Lord...'

A large smooth beach stone was passed round and, as each person held it, he or she thanked God for some blessing.

A piece of rusty barbed wire had been found buried in the sand dunes. The leader held it up, and said a short impromptu prayer for God to forgive us all when we spoil what he has made. The beach-stone circulated again, and each person asked God's forgiveness for something done, or left undone, or spoiled.

The leader held up the driftwood cross and reminded the huddle how hostile the sea can be, and how Jesus' own disciples panicked trying to walk across the water...but Jesus sustained them. Round went the beach-stone again, each person calling out someone or something in danger and asking Jesus' strength and protection.

The leader held up a sprig of gorse, as a symbol of renewed life springing from the desert.

Then came the song – 'Seek ye first the Kingdom of God' – some hummed, some put in the words...it picked up strength as it went along.

After that the Celtic blessing, spoken quietly together, thrice:

> 'Deep peace of the running wave to you
> Deep peace of the flowing air to you
> Deep peace of the quiet earth to you
> Deep peace of the shining stars to you
> Deep peace of the Son of Peace to you.'

Silence – but for plash and flap and screech of gull.

Half an hour's modest offering by amateurs on the land's margin and the edge of wonder. Liturgically unsound in many parts, no doubt, and a bit disjointed – but perhaps it pleased the Creator, even so.

SOME PRACTICAL SUGGESTIONS

Gather together a group of all ages and paint some icons.

You'll need some powder paint...mix it with yolk of an egg – add water and vinegar.

A block of wood...mark out a frame with a nail.

Paint the picture inside the frame...this is the window into heaven.

Decorate it with gold paint and sequins.

Spend time talking together after you've painted your pictures. Put them in some order...make connections...

Light a candle in front of them and sit for a moment in silence.

Use silence and breathing exercises...Breathe in slowly to the count of ten and out to the count of ten...think about the breath of God flowing through you.

It's often useful to give people something to think about, something to look at: pictures, household objects...

The making of a simple wooden cross can often mean a great deal. Two small twigs bound together with a piece of string or wool...Adults and children could help one another in silence...Use them during the intercession time, instead of Palm crosses, at Good Friday services, at Baptism services.

Create opportunities where people can tell stories to one another: traditional stories, their own story, Bible stories...

Children love to take part in stories 'in the round'. One person starts off and then passes the story to the person next to them.

A good way of dealing with narrative Bible stories is to imagine that you are one of the characters. Retell the story from that character's point of view.

Choose a Bible passage and ask people to proclaim its central truth without using words. Have a variety of paper, glue, material, clay, etc. available as well. You'll be amazed how creative people can be...

Make up a group story and have a rule that there are to be no overt religious images and language...you'll be surprised what will happen...

Pantomimes, musicals and drama performances that include all ages can be some of the most spiritual experiences. All you need is an enthusiast. Do it, and see what happens.

Organise a pilgrimage. Invite people of all ages to travel together to a special place. Organise and plan the route, the worship, food, etc., together.

Learn and practise a new technique...if you've never done it before, make the sign of the Cross and think of Christ binding you together...

Use your body in worship...lift up your hands...use movement...

Learn a new hymn and talk together about the words.

Let people of all ages choose their favourite hymns in a 'Songs of Praise' service...ask people why they have chosen the hymn.

Organise a weekend for all ages where you look at an issue that concerns you all. Plan worship around the theme. Spend some time thinking about some common action for the future.

Use pictures, household objects, buildings, trees, in fact anything available, and ask people to make connections between the earthly and heavenly. With a little practice, children can develop astonishing associations...Old Master paintings and Christmas scenes are full of symbolism. Mother Julian saw divine love in a seed: open your eyes and see what you can see.

Use your church. Plan a day or half a day, exploring, using cards and books available (see Resources lists). Gather for lunch or tea, or concluding worship. Give time to talk and share discoveries and thinking.

Have a day of workshops in church and hall. Get local people to organise and lead flower arranging, arts, crafts, music, dance, drama, etc.; include the churchyard if you have one. Choose a theme and use some of the finished work in the worship that day or on the nearest Sunday.

Have an exhibition of people's work and hobbies: writing poetry, tapestry, woodwork, metalwork, needlework, flower arranging, cooking and so on, at Harvest, or as a Thanksgiving patronal festival or dedication time. Link it with the worship.

Plan a Festival of Family – or of Christian Life and Living. Have an exhibition of items on birth, childhood, youth, adult, homes, families, friends, lifestyle and death.

Arrange workshops, groups, talks for parents, children, etc. on baptism, marriage preparation, bereavement, visiting, teenage/parent relationships, conflicts in the home/school/church, society – its pressures, demands, possibilities – adventures of life, and so on.

Consider the homeless in your local area: get some hard information and think about practical help. Discover – and be surprised – by what is already going on in the way of voluntary work, by children as well as adults.

Whenever you have an all-age day or weekend, remember to plan time to reflect and discuss. What has happened – as a whole – to individuals? Stop to think: where do we go? What do we do next? How is this going to affect our worship and life?

A PROGRAMME OF ALL-AGE LEARNING
Often the all-age event in one day is a beginning. It should not be the end of all-age learning in a parish! Consider the ways in which a parish programme for Christian education can be planned with all ages in mind. Start discussions in the PCC – or form in a special group to consider, or have an open meeting.

What is already being done with children and young people?

What opportunities are there for them to get to know a variety of adult Christians?

How often and how much are adults able to share the work with the insights of children?

What strategy could we/do we provide in our parish for the building up of relationships between people of all ages?

How could more people be involved in baptism preparation and follow-up – confirmation preparation and follow-up?

How do we encourage people of all ages to grow in faith and spiritual awareness?

What event, service, experience in the past two years has enabled the individual members of the group to deepen their understanding of their faith?

Possible outcomes of such a meeting and discussion might be:

1. A decision to set up a learning programme that would include the present work being done with children – after it has been studied in detail and possibilities of changes considered.

2. The involvement of children in study groups, Bible study groups, prayer groups already in existence.

3. The involvement of families and individuals in the worship week by week, in planning, taking part in readings, intercessions, welcome, choice of music, hymns, etc. with a coming together for help/training to do this.

4. An annual programme of parish education on a weekly, monthly, seasonal basis –

   e.g. six weeks of group study in Lent in mixed ages, or in separated ages on the same evening or all joining for a final time of discussion or with opportunity on Sundays to share the group's thinking.

   Again, for five weeks before and during Advent – with the possibility of a day of activities as part of the total programme, both in Lent and Advent.

   The *group study* could involve use of videos, films, speakers, discussions, activities, Bible study.

5. A *weekly* programme of study. With the congregational gathering *before* worship to be together, in groups or as a body, for half to three-quarters of an hour – all ages, flexible choice of groups. Alternatively, adult groups at some time as 'Sunday school' and all ages gather for worship together, sharing experiences within the worship.

6. *Once a month* an extended time together on a Sunday to meet for study and worship and *perhaps* a meal together.

7. Use of *festivals* to have a day or half a day together of study and activities on related themes, e.g. Christmas, Easter, Pentecost, Harvest.

8. A weekend away together as a parish – involving study, worship and leisure for all ages together.

9. A programme of study of the church music, prayer, liturgy – as part of the eucharistic Ministry of the Word, or at other times in the week.

10. A gathering of already established groups/clubs in a parish – e.g. Mothers' Union, choir, Sunday school, uniformed organisations – into a planned programme of learning.

    For example, the Mothers' Union could plan a parish day or afternoon/evening on 'Family Life' – or celebrating festivals in the home, or praying as a family, perhaps near to Mothering Sunday. The uniformed organisations could contribute a day of planned activities and skills enabling all ages to join in, concluding with 'camp-fire worship'. The choir could enable others to enjoy the church music in an evening/day of listening, learning, sharing, creating music together and exploring traditional and new music for worship.

11. Different ways of studying the Bible could be explored on 'Bible Sunday' – or in a series of weekly Bible studies for all ages involving drama, guided imagination and other techniques.

12. Groups to learn together about visiting, counselling, welcoming, relationships, could be formed and people of all ages given opportunities and encouragement to use this ministry in the wider community and in the congregation week by week.

13. Links with local schools and colleges could be initiated, established/strengthened and an exchange encouraged between the church and these places.

14. A sharing together of information and experience by church people already heavily involved in community work and service could lead to other opportunities for work and witness, a deepening of understanding and commitment by people to the needs and opportunities locally, nationally, worldwide.

Members of a congregation are often totally unaware of the voluntary work undertaken by so many of their neighbours in the pews. Children need to be enabled to share this and to bring their own enthusiasm and desires to help.

15. A decision could be taken to involve everyone, or families and individuals, in support of and friendship with children and adults before and after baptism. This could include attendance at preparation classes, or visits, or being involved in the preparation. It could mean a programme of annual or biennial services for all baptised in the church. The same could happen for marriage couples.

16. The care of the bereaved could be considered. This might involve a group keeping note of dates for the 'year's mind', or of anniversaries and being especially aware of the need for a visit, prayer, support. The provision of a small 'thanksgiving or memory table' in church where people – including children – can leave flowers at such times is often of value.

17. The possibilities of a 'link' with another parish, in a totally different part of the country, or overseas might be considered. A sharing of learning about each other by letter, photographs, visits could develop. Often an already existing 'missionary' link can be deepened and strengthened through study, prayer and a determined effort to interest others.

SUMMARY OF IDEAS FOR LEARNING TOGETHER
The chapter comments further on the parish education programme that should be planned with all ages in mind, in which all-age events, ecumenical opportunities, peer group sharing, Bible study, prayer, groups, commitment to serve, use of talents, learning in all ways will all play their part.

Additional letters
These are included to help readers to think how they would have replied, and to draw their own conclusions about all-age learning from them.

Ideas for Activities
Page 45: *parachute games* – (see Resource list and *Signposts on the Way*) for further details and ideas.

There are folk in most parishes who, for various reasons, feel as strongly as this. A variety of activities, as outlined in this book, may help them to change their views – but until there is a widespread realisation that we do need our children and each other in our pilgrimage, in our learning, they will continue to grumble and to feel unhappy. No-one promised us that the road would be easy...

7. A Selection of Printed Resources

NB: Not all of these resources were written with all-age occasions in mind, but they contain valuable material which can be readily adapted.

1. IDEAS FOR PROGRAMMES
Starters: On Becoming a Christian. Lyman Coleman and Denny Rydberg. Serendipity Youth Bible Study Series. (Scripture Union)

Know How – Special Events for all the Church Family. Michael Lush. (Scripture Union)

Let's have a Family Day. Mothers' Union Young Families' Dept. (The Mothers' Union, 24 Tufton Street, London SW1P 3RB)

Family Matters. NCEC Project 1989. (National Christian Education Council, Robert Denholm House, Nutfield, Redhill, Surrey RH1 4HW)

Know How – all-age activities for learning and worship. Michael Lush. (Scripture Union)

'Creativity'. Creative Workshops for World Concern. The YMCA's world development agency. (Y Care International, 640 Forest Road, London E17 3DZ)

2. WORSHIP
All Generations. A Handbook for Leaders of Family Worship. (Church House Publishing)

The Child and the Eucharist. A Source Book for Teachers and Clergy. Leslie Francis. (Mayhew McCrimmon)

Helping Children Participate in Holy Communion. Leigh Pope. (The Joint Board of Christian Education, 10 Queen Street, Melbourne, Australia)

Together for Festivals 2 and other 'Together' resource anthologies. (National Society/Church House Publishing)

Know How to Encourage Family Worship. Howard Mellor. (Scripture Union)

Worship in the Round. Patterns of informal and participative worship. (The Joint Board of Christian Education, 177 Collins Street, Melbourne, Australia)

Worship and Outreach. Produced by The Mothers' Union Young Families' Dept.

All Age Worship. Maggie Durran. (Angel Press)

Church Family Worship. Michael Perry. Church Pastoral Aid Society and Jubilate Hymns. (Hodder & Stoughton)

Patterns for Worship. A Report by the Liturgical Commission. (Church House Publishing)

The Iona Community Worship Book and other publications from the Iona Community (Wild Goose Publications, Pearce Institute, 840 Govan Road, Glasgow G51 3UT)

3. ALL-AGE TEACHING

'Learning All Together' Magazine. (Scripture Union, 130 City Road, London EC1V 2NJ)

'Partners in Learning' Magazine. (National Christian Education Council, Robert Denholm House, Nutfield, Redhill, Surrey RH1 4HW)

'Together' Magazine. (The National Society, Church House, Westminster, London SW1P 3NZ)

4. GENERAL

How to Pray with your Children. (Veritas Family Resources, Veritas House, 7/8 Lower Abbey Street, Dublin 1)

The Religious Potential of the Child. The description of an experience with children from ages 3-6. Sofia Cavelletti. (Paulist Press, New Jersey, USA)

Jesus and the Children. Biblical resources for study and preaching. Hans-Reudi Weber. (NCEC)

Seen and Heard. New possibilities for Children in the Church. David Merritt. (The Joint Board of Christian Education, 10 Queen Street, Melbourne, Australia)

Family Ministry. A practical guide for a teaching church. Joe Leonard. (Scripture Union)

Your Child and Religion. Johanna Klink. (Northumberland Press Ltd., Gateshead)

Helping Children to Pray. Ruth Cardell. (Grail Publishing)

Children in the Way. A Report to General Synod from the Board of Education. (National Society/Church House Publishing)

Children and God. Ron Buckland. (Scripture Union)

Let's Celebrate. Tony Castle. (Hodder and Stoughton)

We Always put a Candle in the Window. Marjorie Carnelley. (National Society/Church House Publishing)

Homemade Christians. Nancy Marrocco. (Collins/Novalis)

Making Contact. Christian Nurture, Family Worship and Church Growth. Leslie Francis. (Collins)

The Child in the Church. (British Council of Churches)

Will our Children have Faith? John Westerhoff III. (Seabury Press, USA)

A Pilgrim People. Learning through the Christian Year. John Westerhoff III. (Seabury Press, USA)

Becoming Adult, becoming Christian. James Fowler. (Harper & Row)

Bringing up Children in the Christian Faith. John Westerhoff III. (Winston Press, USA)

Help, There's a Child in my Church. Peter Graystone. (Scripture Union)

Children Finding Faith. Frances Bridger. (Scripture Union)

Let's have Children in Church. (The Mothers' Union Young Families' Dept.)

5. DIOCESAN PUBLICATIONS

Steps along the Way. Salisbury Diocesan Education Office, Audley House, 97 Crane Street, Salisbury, SP1 2QA.

Pilgrims. Programme Ideas for children, young people, adults, all ages together. York Diocesan Education Office, Church House, Ogleforth, York, YO1 2JE.

Family Services. Gloucester Diocesan Education Office, Church House, College Green, Gloucester, GL1 2LY.

Planning All-Age Events. Manchester Diocesan Council of Education, Diocesan Church House, 90 Deansgate, Manchester, M3 2GJ.

'Children in the Way' – What Next? Newcastle Diocesan Board of Education, Church House, Grainger Park Road, Newcastle-upon-Tyne, NE4 8SX.

'All Age' Pack. Lichfield Diocesan Board of Education, St Mary's House, The Close, Lichfield, WS13 7LD.

Signposts along the Way. Midland Dioceses. (Available from the Revd Peter Privett, The Vicarage, Dilwyn, Hereford, HE4 8HW)

Exploring a Church and Churchyard (30 cards). Children's Officer, General Synod Board of Education, Church House, Westminster, London SW1P 3NZ.